# MAYOR PETE 2020

### Written by Larry Corkins

### Copyright©LarryCorkins2019

# DEDICATED

To all people who believe that everyone has purpose and worth. There is no one person that is greater than another. This book represents the heart and soul of the best of what America has to offer. Mayor Pete Buttigieg of South Bend, Indiana is running for President on the values and belief in GOD that were taught to him by his parents and his church. There is a saying that goes "You can't keep a good man down." While I am writing this, I believe that you cannot keep a good Presidential candidate down and Mayor Pete is as good as they come. This book is dedicated to him also and mainly, because I know him to be a hard worker who gets things done that make sense. If Mayor Pete is elected President of the United States of America, I have no doubt that he will work just as hard to serve the people of this great country proudly and with the dignity that has been lacking in the White House since the current occupant took over.

# ACKNOWLEDGMENTS

First, I must as always and have in all of my books, thank and give praise to my LORD and Savior Jesus Christ. GOD is good all the time! I would also like to acknowledge Mayor Pete Buttigieg for being a bright light in a dark world. Jesus did not tell us to hate our brothers and sisters, but to love everyone no matter what!

## Chapter 1

Being President of the United States of America is one of the hardest, if not THE hardest jobs in the world. It should never be taken lightly, as the President has to have the best interest of all of our citizens. That has not been happening since the latest occupant of the White House took over. We have a chance now to rectify that situation. We must all get out and vote though. If we do not vote, Trump will win again because Republicans almost always vote for their candidate. Democrats have a history of staying home and not voting. The times are very crucial right now. America is not great, but full of hate! That is what Trump really stands for anyway, HATE! He is always touting 'Make America Great Again', but all he is showing is 'Make America Hate Again'. Racism has roared back, because the President himself is racist, as evident by how he reacted to the Ku Klux Klan's endorsement for President during the last election. He was told to denounce them, but his response was that he did not know enough about their organization. It is not an organization, but a hate group!

It is time to stop condemning people and learn to live together in peace and harmony. That is what we will get if we vote in Mayor Pete as our next President.

Compassion and caring for everyone. It is

that important. America cannot move

forward and become the great country we

want it to be if we keep going down the road

we are going. Some people claim it already

is what they want it to be. Those are the

racist people who voted for Trump and think

that all of his hate-filled tweets are okay.

It is definitely not okay to spew hate

at others and even cause people who hang

on your every word to send death threats to

people like Rep. Omar, just because she is

Muslim. Even Vice President Pence has

been showing hate towards Mayor Pete for

being gay. These people do this all in the name of GOD.

Maybe they did not read the Bible correctly. While they are so self-righteous and holier than thou, they do not even realize that Jesus said HE wants us all to love each other. As a matter of fact, someone asked HIM what He was here to do? Was HE here to change the Commandments? Jesus told him that HE was not here to change the Ten Commandments, but to add to them. HE said that we must love GOD the Father and love each other. President Trump is following that advice, NOT AT ALL! And now Vice President Pence is so holy that he wants to slam Mayor Pete. Is he without sin? Jesus said for those without sin to cast the first stone. There are a lot of stones being thrown around by the President and Vice President. I guess they have no sins!

I rode by Macedonia Missionary Baptist Church a couple of days ago and I liked the sign they had up on their board outside. It said, "GOD MADE YOU THE WAY YOU ARE SO THAT HE COULD USE YOU AS HE PLANNED." I truly believe that to be correct. You see this life is just one big test for the next life in Heaven…or hell for some. While people are judging themselves to be without sin and others with great sins, Jesus already knows what's up with all of us. And guess what??? HE loves us just the same!!!

## Chapter 2

Mayor Pete has changed a lot of things in South Bend. Made the city grow again. Yes, he is the youngest Mayor we have ever had and he will be the youngest President if he wins, but he has a common sense approach that just does exactly that- make sense.

When Pete was elected Mayor, he jumped right in and made choices that benefited the city as a whole. He will do the same thing for the country as well. Isn't it about time that we have a real common sense approach to running this country instead of the chaos that Trump has created?

Trump has stoked a fire of racism that has divided this country more than any time in our history since the Civil Rights Movement of the sixties. The Ku Klux Klan and Neo-Nazis have a voice again thanks to Trump! Don't forget that when the so-called White Nationalists (Supremacists) aka KKK got into a brawl with black people and others who are not racist in the Carolinas Trump said there was blame on both sides, not wanting to blame the KKK for what happened. If Trump is not a Klan member himself, then he is most certainly a KKK sympathizer!

While Trump is attacking people of color, mostly Mexicans, Vice President Mike Pence has taken it upon himself to condemn gay people, starting with South Bend's Mayor, Pete Buttigieg.

Why is it so acceptable for Trump and Pence to attack people? People are just people and no one is above GOD. Get over your fears and phobia's and follow the will of GOD, which is to love each other. You so-called Christians need to stop playing GOD. Let GOD do HIS own job and you do yours. Your job is not to judge others, but to treat everyone like Jesus treats you.

As Mayor Pete goes forward with his campaign, he will encounter many people who want to condemn him for being gay, but Pete Buttigieg is the kind of guy who can handle it. The way that he keeps his cool when others rage against him for being different from any candidate for President that we have ever known gives you a glimpse of what kind of cool he will have while being President of the United States.

Since some people like Vice President Mike Pence want to judge Pete Buttigieg using the Bible to supposedly prove their point, Jesus told me that HE wants us to learn to live together and love each other the best we can. HE also wants us to leave judgments to Him as it is HIS job and not ours. Just because the Bible says that homosexuals will go to hell does not mean that anyone is supposed to hate them in anticipation of such a thing. The Bible also says that all liars will go to hell. It says that all thieves and murderers and adulterers and do I have to go on?

Okay, so if you believe that GOD can not forgive and will not forgive, you are sadly mistaken. HE forgives all who ask in Jesus' name. You have to really mean it though. And let's talk about those liars who are going to hell. Get real! Everyone who has ever lived has lied about something. So if that is true then all of you haters are going to hell! If you don't get it yet, check this out. You have lied about someone having a birthday party or getting a present. You just sealed your fate to go to hell. That is what the Bible says.

You still don't get it? The Bible does not lie, but you do. The Bible says these things, but you already know that no matter what your sin is, you can still get GOD'S forgiveness. Everyone is going to hell before they go to GOD and accept Jesus as their personal Savior. That is how it really is. Anyone who claims that someone, anyone is going to hell is playing GOD. Jesus said

love each other. HE did not say you don't

have to if you are holier than thou. And how

are you holier than Jesus?

Can we finally get past this and look

at Mayor Pete for the kind of person he is

and the kind of President he would be if he

wins the nomination?

## Chapter 3

Let's talk about foreign affairs. How will Mayor Pete handle that? How does Trump handle that? Not very well when he thinks that the nut case in North Korea is having a love affair with him. Trump did tweet that. Remember? And Trump is not doing very well when he treats Putin like a rock star and Trump is his number one girl school fan. You do know who Putin is, right? Russia's leader does not care about us.

So how is Trump doing? Let's see, North Korea has started testing missiles again, and they are aimed at the U.S. and Putin has threatened to send missiles that go the speed of sound if we want a war. When did we say we wanted a war? And aren't you, Putin supposed to be cool with Trump? Guess not. Russia only meddled in our election to make sure Hilary Clinton lost, because she was a threat to Russia. Putin did not care who won as long as it was not Hilary.

Trump is running around bragging that there was no collusion between him and Russia, but that does not change the fact that Russia still meddled in our election and made sure Trump won. Otherwise Trump would have never been President and the

Republicans would be trying to unseat Hilary Clinton.

I brought all of that up to say this: Trump is an embarrassment to the United States of America. He looks like a fool to other countries. He says the most ridiculous things and does them too. He does not know what he is doing overseas and has never been in the military. Still he hates on a war hero, John McCain.

Pete is a former Navy Intelligence Officer, serving in the United States Navy Reserves and rising to the rank of lieutenant. He was deployed to the War in Afghanistan in 2014, while he was Mayor of South Bend.

Mayor Pete is far more qualified to handle foreign situations, especially those of military nature than the one in the Oval Office right now or even his rivals for the Democratic nomination. He is a proven leader and a War Veteran.

Chapter 4

It takes intelligence to be a GOOD
President. It also takes common sense and
compassion for others. Pete Buttigieg has all
of these. You will never hear him say that a
group of people are rapists and murderers.
You will never hear him say that John
McCain is not a War Hero because he was
captured by the enemy. You will never hear
him say that he is having a love relationship
with our enemy, like North Korea. You will
never see him act like the leader of Russia is
the greatest thing since sliced bread.

You will NOT even read that he said
something bad about anyone just because he

can. And you will never hear Peter say that the people who are being hated on are the blame for what might happen to them. Heck, you won't even hear of President Pete not wanting to help part of our own territory like Puerto Rico after they were ravaged by a hurricane, all the while blaming them for their own fate. And you surely will not ever hear President Pete tell another country that they are going to pay for a wall that they do not want.

There are a lot of other things that I could say that Pete would not do, but I think I should focus more on what Pete will do. The first thing that I believe President Pete would do is give the United States of America a sigh of relief. Relief that now common sense will prevail. Relief that compassion and caring for American lives will be back in the Oval Office. Relief that people of all colors and sexual orientations and nationalities will once again be able to live side by side with each other without the racist tones and attitudes that have plagued us since Trump took office. Relief that when part of our country needs us the most, we will be there for them.

It is a disgrace that a President can and does distance himself from doing his job of treating every American citizen with pride and dignity. We are a melting pot of cultures and ideas. We are a mixture of all the wonderful nationalities, races, sexual orientations and diversities that GOD will allow. Pete Buttigieg knows that and respects the nature of that.

There seems to have been a thought process in this country that young people don't know anything, but this is a new day and Mayor Pete represents a new thought process that says young people can and are affective in doing more than expected by much older but not necessarily wiser people. This is our future and Pete is the future of our country as much as anyone is.

If you want to know about Pete's level of intelligence, then you may be interested to know this: Pete Buttigieg was educated and is a graduate of Harvard University and Oxford University, having attended Pembroke College, Oxford on a Rhodes Scholarship. He also worked for McKinsey and Company (a management strategy consulting firm) from 2007 to 2010. He was elected Mayor of South Bend, Indiana on 2011 and again in 2015. In 2013, Pete won the GovFresh's Mayor of the Year award.

Pete was valedictorian of his high school senior class at St. Joseph High

School in South Bend. He was a recipient

that year of a first prize for the JFK Profiles

in Courage Essay Contest awarded by the

John F. Kennedy Library in Boston. When

Pete went to Boston to accept the award he

met Caroline Kennedy and other members

of the Kennedy family. Pete had written

about the integrity and political courage

demonstrated by U.S. Congressman Bernie

Sanders of Vermont.

Mayor Pete majored in history and

literature at Harvard where he was president

of the Harvard Institutes of Politics Study

Advisory Committee and he worked on the

institutes annual study of youth attitudes on

politics. Pete wrote his undergraduate thesis on the influence of puritanism on U. S. foreign policy. Pete graduated from Harvard in 2005 and was the recipient of a Rhodes Scholarship. In 2007, Pete received first-class honors in philosophy, politics and economics from Pembroke College, Oxford.

While at Harvard, Pete was president of the Harvard Institute of Politics Student Advisory Committee. He worked on the Institute's annual study of youth attitudes on politics. Pete wrote his undergraduate thesis on the influence of puritanism on U. S. foreign policy as reflected in Graham Greene's novel The Quiet American.

Pete worked in Washington D. C. for former U. S. Secretary of Defense William Cohen's international strategic consulting firm, The Cohen Group from 2004 to 2005. Pete also spent several months working on Senator John Kerry's 2004 presidential campaign, where he was a policy and research specialist.

## Chapter 5

Mayor Pete Buttigieg's platform includes, but not limited to: Universal Healthcare, reducing income inequality, pro-environmental policies, dialogue and cooperation between the Democratic Party and organized labor, universal background checks for firearms purchases, federal legislation that would ban job discrimination against LGBT people, and preserving the Deferred Action for Childhood Arrivals program for children of immigrants. Mayor Pete also supports overturning Citizens United and ending gerrymandering.

When Pete became Mayor of South Bend, the FBI was investigating the South Bend Police Chief for wire tapping his own officers. Turns out a police officer who was no longer with the department had left his phone recording calls and a lot of things were said against the Police Chief who was black. The officers who were recorded were white and were making racial slurs against the Chief.

Mayor Pete fired the Police Chief when the FBI informed him of the investigation. Since the Police Chief was black, the African-American community took it personally without knowing any facts at all. The black community did not know how to take it but have since moved on realizing that Mayor Pete is doing a good job for the city as a whole. At least most people have moved on. You cannot ever say everyone is on board no matter what the issue is.

Mayor Pete has revitalized the downtown area of South Bend. Some say that he has not done enough for the urban areas, but I believe that Mayor Pete started where the city had been dead for some time; downtown. He has already started to make improvements to other areas of the city, but now that he is running for President people think he has forgotten about them. This is not true as best I can tell, because I see the street crews putting in sidewalks and new trees along the residential streets where I live every day now. That was ordered by the Mayor, I am sure.

As the old saying goes, "Rome was not built in a day." Neither can the revitalization of a city. Now even though Mayor Pete is on the campaign trail, he still gets things done in the Bend, as some of us call it.

Chapter 6

There are many good candidates running for
President of the United States, so why
should you vote for Mayor Pete? Pete
Buttigieg knows how to run a city. Most of
the other Democratic candidates do not have
experience running a city. Running a
country is a bigger version of that. Here are
some Presidents who had the experience of
running a smaller version of government,
although it was as Governor are: President
Jimmy Carter, Ronald Reagan, and Bill
Clinton.

What about foreign affairs and
policy? Pete Buttigieg was a Navy Reserve

officer and even had experience in the War in Afghanistan. Do any of the other candidates have military experience? Pete studied foreign policies and solutions.

What about when an emergency happens to one of our cities, states or territories? Trump has not responded well to those types of emergencies, but someone with more compassion and caring will do a much better job. Pete Buttigieg is that someone. The United States still owes it to Puerto Rico, which is our own territory, to give them everything they need to come back from the devastation they encountered.

That will not happen until a Democrat takes over the Oval Office.

The divisiveness that has come about since Trump took office is deplorable. What is more deplorable is the fact that Donald Trump encourages the hatred that is going on. He brings it to the forefront every time he tweets a nasty message directed to anyone and everyone he does not like. It is time for a change.

YOU matter, so don't just sit and do nothing. Vote Trump out! If Mayor Pete is not the one for you, then vote for another Democrat, but whatever you do…VOTE!!!

# ABOUT THE WRITER

Larry Corkins has written several books.

Some of his most notable books include:

JESUS, I AM

ROYAL WOMEN

YOU ARE A MASTERPIECE

JESUS' ETERNAL MESSAGE

OBAMA 44

TRUMPed, The White House Gamble

LeBron, The King James of the NBA

And his latest and first book of Fiction:

BIANCA RENEE

And be on the lookout for his next fiction

book: ROAD RAGE KILLER (out this

summer)

All books can be found on AMAZON.COM